cancer
songs

cancer
songs

Richard Sommer

Carolyn Marie Souaid, Editor

EDITIONS

Cover design by Doowah Design.
Cover photo of Richard Sommer by Jonathan J. Sommer.

This book was printed on Ancient Forest Friendly paper.
Printed and bound in Canada by Marquis Book Printing Inc.

We acknowledge the support of The Canada Council for the Arts and the Manitoba Arts Council for our publishing program.

"The Real World," "The Cancers," "Crystals," and "The Secret Garden" first appeared in Poetry Quebec, Issue #7, March 2011. www.poetry-quebec.com.

Library and Archives Canada Cataloguing in Publication

Sommer, Richard
        Cancer songs / Richard Sommer.

Poems.
ISBN 978-1-897109-54-0

        I. Title.

PS8587.O44C36 2011   C811'.54   C2011-902302-4

Signature Editions
P.O. Box 206, RPO Corydon, Winnipeg, Manitoba, R3M 3S7
www.signature-editions.com

*For my children & grandchildren
& especially my wife Vicki Tansey,
for loving kindness & loyalty in a dark time.*

Foreword: Difficult Celebrations

Perhaps the title of these poems should have been something like "Difficult Celebrations" because they were, no question. Not made much easier for noticing that many people going through a cancer experience were having a much harder time of it than I was. I relied heavily on the idea that one's state of mind can affect the progress of the disease, and kept my mood upbeat throughout the treatment I underwent. I figured I would win either way: if I was going to cure and heal, it would probably help me to be awake and joyful, and if it was going to kill me, I would have used my remaining days sharply and perceptively. The recurrence of my cancer after radiation and hormone treatment has somewhat damaged my faith in this psychosomatic connection, but not entirely. My cancer may or may not be cured, but what I most need now is to heal.

Nobody is cured of life itself, which ends. But many of us are given the means to heal, to become whole and a part of the life around us, all of us sailing through the space/time intersections allotted us. Call it luck or blessing or what you will, the awesome fortune of having been called out of all the molecules in the universe to become a witness to all this, even if it took a possibly lethal disease to bring this fact to my consciousness, fills me with gratitude and awe. Whether I lived or died, when that was for a time in question, diminished in importance by comparison with this incredible fact that I was here at all.

The poems were written shortly before, during, and after my diagnosis and treatment. They are not necessarily 'about' the cancer or my response to it – they were part of that response – and look out from a world that includes such difficulties as cancer, and as it was coloured for me by what I went through.

In the course of my illness, courage to persist & see life out seemed to come to me out of the air, out of sunlight & rain, the affections & generosity of people & animals around me. If these poems can help anyone with cancer draw on this kind of courage, they will have been worth writing.

Richard Sommer
Frelighsberg, April 2011

Dreaming

Same time, same place, same frame
of same screened window
looking out on garden against rock wall

rose-pink blooms on long stalks
nameless to me,
nameless arching ferns,

a patch of spread palmate leaves
blazing & yellowing into autumn,
nameless to me, nameless.

Where have I been,
what have I been thinking
while all this has been going on?

Have I wasted my life?

Memento

The stuff lingers,
even if you can't any longer
tell what it is, but feel it there

taking many forms:
slide of oyster over the palate
deep musk of the other's groin

crash of ocean with hint of sand in your eye
dog tongue licking your instep & toes
Bach lifting a cathedral from within

the tick of a clock in an afternoon room
& glory in backlit autumn leaves.
You don't want to leave this.

You never wanted to leave this
knowing leaving was always part of the bargain
& any time now it could be time.

But as you observed, the stuff lingers.

Sort Of Sonnet

Today to the Sherbrooke hospital for a biopsy
so it's hard to think of writing when
in a couple of hours a surgeon I haven't yet met
will guide a sampling needle into my innermost in.

I'd better get off this verse
while I still can
& do something useful, Tai Chi or even getting to work.
The calories it takes, just trying to be a man!

Get the circulation going, breathe deeply,
all the stuff they say in yoga.
Or shout like Stentor, whose voice reputedly
could fell an ox at ten paces & never ruffle his own toga.

No, yelling my panic would disturb the neighbours
& I already owe them big favours.

Who's In Charge Of Blessing Here?

Whenever the geese call overhead
a part of you would rise & fly with them
if you could & still be human

& that's the catch, to be
both in & outside the human at once,
human a roiled ocean of antipathies & sympathies:

to be able to imagine yourself the other
to be able to take the other in
until there is no other —

what else is there?
Just that & playing flute music all afternoon
in dappled summer sun

or burying your face in your dog's cold fur
smelling of spruce needles & snowflakes
& letting yourself breathe in there

just belonging to everybody.

For You

The sinuous fit of wing with air
of fin with water flow
is the god I know

of tints to feed the eye
of wine to deepen the taste
& so sometimes your eyes

hold me in their olive depth
& in your eyes you hold me always
though I can hardly lift mine

to meet their searching
but feel held in your eyes,
really held.

Diagnosis

Perhaps I could persuade myself to remember past lives.
Maybe I could fool myself into believing in a future.
Could but won't, I'll wait for good evidence.

Today I see a doctor who will probably tell me
I will soon die if I don't let them
cut and/or burn and/or poison me

leaving me incontinent and/or impotent
temporarily or forever
& this is really happening & to me.

Today the test results come back
& will find most likely against, or otherwise
find an unlikely reprieve & a freedom to be free

I can't just now even begin to imagine.

The Day After

The day after I learn I have cancer:
brushing Phoebe's sumptuous fur,
a waterfall of white, gold & russet
shifting & cascading with her breath.

Listening to a harpsichord
finessing the *Inventions*
in aerial interlace with swallows
over the pond in twilight, the light golden.

Seeing this in the mind's eye,
acknowledging the first seeing,
the rustle & thrum of their passing,
a glimpse of tiny bellies & underwings

whistling past & away golden
(sharp black speck eyes inspecting me
as they bank away)
& all this, to remember to remember this:

a wet gnarled rock's hieroglyphs,
creaky voices of distant geese,
an opened rosemary jar,
transparent & illuminated. Floating.

The Real World

Obstinately wordless
this morning is.

Pale crystal sunlight
cracks & breaks everywhere.

Rain last night, but now
ice crunches under boot.

Phoebe is at her ease,
lying on the driveway ice.

All seems untranslatable.
No one thing stands for any other.

No thoughts that might become words.
No words taking sudden fire

so nothing is what's happening
& you could get lost in there.

The Love

Long talks with V. with M. with Mother with Jack
with Phoebe in the tongue of dogs
with Luna in the feline words of touch,

from every direction the love I will need
if I'm going to heal comes in.
Maybe it's the love, the knowledge of love

surrounding & holding & around me.
Nobody can take my place in the coming dark,
they can only hold & surround me & they do

with love from the forever before I was born.

The Cancers

Too many issues circling in your head to make this easy:
the cancer in your groin, the cancer in your native land,
the growths spreading, blotching the globe,

the globe most of us imagine or deduce
when we watch a sail's white belly sink below
horizons at sea, but to see is to believe

& only a chosen few have seen our sphere directly,
& seen further that it's ours beyond ourselves
& we are the ones must heal it

or the cancers will grow over us, tangle us
in nets of competition for water & food & space
tendrils of unlimited growth to choke & close off

& use against each other in poisonous ways
that in retrospect will seem obvious.
Do you want a list?

Crisis

Crashing discords can smash through
any tie that binds
lovers in the darkness of the blues
to the memory of their sins & sighs.

Could be death, the wind, the sea
or none of them
yet the crash that ensues
changes everything to a hymn

sung over the deep sleep of stones
all unknowable to anyone.

Unexpected

The angularity of now
the unexpected intrusions
the corners that stick out
the sudden projections

catch you in the eye, or would
except you predict & duck
& learn to improvise an ode
to your mind intent on each fact

taking joy in each quick jump
the world around you takes
when for one reason or another
it stops rhyming, a hiatus gapes

open to starlit power of space & so
what you've been looking for
is here in the heart of the unexpected where
all words fall short.

Cold

Cold in the bones this morning
off early to med appointment & groceries
& the car takes a long time warming up.

Sixteen below, it says,
the bones say the same, it's all the same
whether with pain or delight

it's a rightness & seeing
an exactness of wing in flight
of things coming alive in your sight

the being in being alive wherever
& whoever you are is who you are
& when you look around you

everything is new & different & the same
in its own blessing of particularity,
each glint of snow calling you.

Real Life

Last day of a difficult year
but no diminishment, nothing to complain of.
I'm seventy good years into it

& if any were darkened, it was me
brought it on, no choice but to choose
& maybe choose wrong

but this is no apology, no accusation.
All of it has brought me to happiness here,
this vivid new ecstasy of danger

announces the beginning of my end,
& in the deeps of each moment now
real life begins.

Chickadees & finches at the feeder
fluttering & nudging & poking after seed,
so lovely, my teachers!

Someone To Watch Over Me

Out this window
melting snow & ice
in treacherous cahoots

to bring down
any vertical biped who dares
walk upon it.

Phoebe arrives,
a small wet stick hanging
from the corner of her jaw,

plunks herself down
in the melting slush &
gnaws softly upon it,

tail to the south wind,
turns her tricolor muzzle
into this warm air

content to breathe it in
& taste the snow
between her paws.

Surveys horizon.
She's watching out for me

I realize.

Morning

Outside, all white & melting.
Under snow weight
branches bend & creak.

Some crack & break,
some bend down so long
they never rise again.

From here, a mind
slaps metaphor on this,
looks out on snow

& thinks too much, thinks now,
some let the wind shake off the snow,
rest then rise to the light again.

The Dance Of Turning Over In Bed

Your goblins are off somewhere gobbling
in the dark of last night
still trying to scare themselves sillier
thus letting you get a little sleep.

Yesterday pain from a long damaged shoulder
merged with arthritis in toe & finger & thumb
along with a neck crick & periodontal pain
from a recent root canal that got infected

all converging in an ibuprofen fog
with a swelling prostate to ache & irritate
bladder & rectum & groin
into visits to a cold lonely toilet

all night long ad nauseam ad infinitum
all further excited by initial testosterone flare-up
from the hormone therapy
you're getting for your cancer.

All these haven't directly helped you
love the world or live in it
but they haven't stopped you so far either.
You love most what you have to leave.

Joy

Chickadee just landed on a twig
outside my window in crackling cold,
hangs upside down among long thorns,

looks around. Flies away.

Joy is where I find it:
a shaft of sunlight illuminates
my wet dishrag.

Each has its own kind of gleam,
porcelain & snow
& a white cat watching birds through glass.

You Consider Leaving

If it weren't for the radiance of children
lighting their beginnings from within
if it weren't for the luminous sex of the young

if it weren't for the rainbow of skin colours
if it weren't for the rainbow of skin
if it weren't for the rainbow

if it weren't for the dawn
for the return of relentless light
your life would be only grey & pitiless

& you would be glad to be gone

Enough

Coarse & fibrous it tastes to me now,
as six months after going off all those things
like red meat, alcohol, animal fats

I sneak a tiny piece of chicken off Victoria's plate.
It's, how shall I say, disappointing
though engulfed in Vicki's special sauce

which after I have licked it off
leaves no aftertaste
in the soft hen muscle wood I chew.

And swallow too, but no more, thank you.

Flash

Like sudden flash recall
late night loud noise from a bar
a long way down a hot street long ago,

or glints in a vast slow wave
before it hits the shore.
The wave is you & the shore is death

yet both are still only metaphor
for that flash of understanding how much you lose
when you lose mind & breath.

Ides Of March

While I write this
my wonderful father

a book in his pocket, probably
some technical manual or other,

is being driven to the Mayo Clinic
through melting fields

for a second opinion on surgery
for leaky valves at eighty-nine,

his present life miserable.
My brother David is driving the two of them,

Jack & Ida. Even in my imagination
I can't begin to know what they mean to one another.

No matter, I belong with them, driving through
those brown & white Minnesota fields towards truth.

Curious
(for Astride)

The implant device is a cross between
a horse syringe & a gun.

She holds it behind her back.
Don't look, she says. Why not? I say.

Take my word for it, she says.
Just don't look.

Who am I to say, so I don't look &
the thing goes THUNG

& I wish I'd looked.

Choosing Treatments

Easy to think Republican American,
that the current cancers are foreign invaders
so you could call it a war, on cancer.

Then up one notch in intelligence
to the notion of cancer as betrayal from within,
a rebellion at the very core of who you are,

you doing yourself in & so on.
(But if your deepest desire is to die
then why undergo treatment?)

So on to the theory of molecular glitch,
that the genes that clean up the errors
get tired & old & don't catch them all anymore

so cells with terminators turned off
grow & grab sugar & proteins & minerals & grow
& spill wrong code into the body's rivers,

a bureaucratic oversight of sorts
requiring cover-up & clean-up afterwards.
Then there are theories of resonance,

body-mind reverberating like a bell
so if you think hard enough about it
you can get it to go away.

For this the evidence is anecdotal & scattered.
If you rely on this alone for treatment
expect on average to be pretty quick dead.

No telling what to think or do.
Do it all or nothing as you choose.
What counts is here already all around you.

Crystals

Morning after long night's rain then freeze
the steady rain sound a part of sleep

& now as I close
the back door behind me

tiny crystals scattered on the ground
wake up to light or spirit or dharma or a god or

whatever you want to call it; in any case
I am stepping carefully among them.

Sunday At Home

My last free day before I get sucked
into radiotherapy

& become the treatment.
Haven't yet packed up to go

but I'll get interested tomorrow.
Today I'd like to be

as much like any ordinary day
as it can be.

Waking, making tea, feeding the dog & cats
sitting still with unlined notebook

open to the empty page
waiting for it to fill of its own

doing the Form which is empty
until I fill it

eating the food I usually eat
working on ordinary jobs like this writing,

walking, raking leaves
casual talk between us, smiles,
the light brush of lips on a bent nape,
sleep & love, I'll try for that

& fill all the ordinary things
with the light they leave as they

slip away from me & are going,
endlessly going & are gone.

Radiotherapy

Today it begins:
I'm in to the city with my luggage,
all my baggage, all kinds.

Just now, the white cat Luna
crossed a lawn full of the lace
of sun & intricate branch shadows

each laying its finger & bar of smudge
softly across her back, smoothing it,
leaving no trace as she moved on.

Watching her saunter across
new grass & old leaves,
I watch a billion years

of still evolving grace.
My eyes take her in.
I won't see her again

for five days anyway,
time for me to hunger after grace,
all kinds of grace.

Calling My Name

Sitting in the waiting room of radiology
waiting for the doctor's visit.

They'll be calling my name any minute now
so these words may stop before they can go —

the receptionists are beautiful, beautiful the nurses
beautiful even the patients in their particular miseries

the lined faces, the terrible head scabs & stitches
the wasted to bone, no hopes, no fears

this incredible human system responding
to all these sufferings, suffering itself, just the suffering.

I'm beginning to understand what I am a part of,
& what this cancer was at the heart of

& while I'm steaming in an anti-hormone hot flash
I'm overtaken with strange happiness,

the waiting room around me is a vision
& I am completely here, wonder of wonders

& hear my name called.
I have to go. Be well.

Got To Say

Nausea this morning, upped a little mucus,
that was all. Banana I just ate however
stayed down. Mystery & paradox.

Maybe it was the spinach pie
devoured on the fly from that Metro deli.
Got to say, changes your world view.

Those poets of nausea had a point:
the light is glare, things stab at the eye,
I push gorge down & again push down

& maybe after a quart of redbush tea
am feeling better, thank you
though got to say

my first thought was the radiation.

The Cardinals

The cardinals are there to hear, these days, not see.
The other day a red flash takeoff & escape into green,
far off in the brush & gone

but then there she was ten feet away
muted mate to the male's absent fire
glowing softly in a veil of leaves

then springing away
the branch left empty & quivering.
Somewhere her beak, her one brilliance,

parts the air, but not here.
All that's left is a torn bit of memory,
a red blur in the mind

oh yes & the dream that night
of cardinals whistling over
my mother's sister's grave.

I don't know which is true.
I don't know why my beautiful aunt disappeared.
I don't know why any of us do, but we do.

The Entrance

Hanging around a hospital hallway
waiting for my ride,
watching the glacial progress of the old

teetering & trembling over their walkers
I see suffering everywhere in the hall,
spilling from examination rooms,

silent & waiting in the waiting rooms.
I am seeing young men & women egg-bald
covered in wigs & hats & brave bandanas

push wheeled May-poles festooned with bottles & tubes
& I am entering an elevator & standing beside a gurney
that carries a hairless, fleshless scarred living skull

grinning out from an unreachable place
& our eyes meet for a second, unbearably
but somehow neither of us looks away

unwilling to surrender to this glimpse
of what might be the lost truth
we both crave & fear,

yet unwilling to let it go, either.
His eyes are browless & sharp, a bird's.
We have nothing & everything in common.

The elevator doors slide open,
the gurney gets stuck on the threshold rut
& I help the orderly push.

Pushed Into Playing For Them

Gave a lecture/demo/concert on flute tonight
for seventeen of the residents, mostly women,
all with one cancer or another.

Both flutes behaved themselves,
sometimes ecstatically
& I've been practicing recently, so

gave as good a sound as I had in me
for these brave & hurting women
& we all shared it like old wine.

Diary

What happened to yesterday? Too busy to notice. Put room in
order, packed for weekend, downtown for radiotherapy zap,
then by Métro to Berri-UQAM, thence to bus station, taking
bus to Sutton, Vicki picking me up, home for supper, not much
appetite & afterwards lay down on couch. Very tired & a little
ill. Covered up. Soon to bed. V. very kind & understanding, her
touch loving.

You dream a knocking at the door
you get up & find slippers & robe
& on the way out step on Phoebe's paw (sorry, Phoeb)
unlock & open & nothing's there.

Somehow you know if you step out into that spring air
it will turn to cold rain & wind
but if you go back in & lock up again
it will have come in with you.

That's one trouble with opening doors then shutting them.

The Butterflies

To say that everything obeys the laws of nature
is to impose a metaphor of obedience & law
on a mere uniformity of response in objects.

Holding & letting go a pebble, it drops every time
(except in wind tunnels, magnetic fields, space, of course)
but obeying laws has nothing to do with the stars.

It is human invention, obeying/disobeying & laws.
It has to do with a group's perception of its safety.
It has no basis in the orbits of planets, regular or irregular.

We invent what we need,
call it fiction or adaptation,
things implicit in the Big Bang Moment.

A troop of pre-school children
wanders by me in the Jardin botanique
each in identical flowered aprons

each holding to a rope connecting to their teacher
who constantly watches & counts
the upturned round faces & their wondering

at flowers they pass,
at released huge blue iridescent wings
of hundreds of butterflies overhead

sailing above their uptilted luminous gazes
then folding to brown dangerous eyes
on a twig.

The children hold on to their rope
but look up & around them.
The catch in my breath

may be just another fiction.
Anyway,
it doesn't obey me.

Anniversary

Fatigue & diarrhea & a touch of nausea
over the weekend, Vicki so looking forward
to our anniversary

(yesterday that was) but instead
filled in signatures on our income tax returns
& wrote cheques to various governments

though touched often in passing,
stopped for hugs to feel us breathe together,
warmth of her against me & with me

as necessary as the life I endure this for.

The Mirror

In the minibus waiting for my ride home,
the rear-view mirror frames
a bent woman, neck thrown forward
parallel to the ground

trying in the wind to sip coffee from a paper cup,
stub of a sheltered cigarette in her other hand
while a Sufi song of prayer plays on our radio.
I hear it. She cannot, yet the Beloved is with her,

I see this even in her reflection.

A Long Wait

Pushed out of the double room I had to myself
into a single with a shared two-door bathroom
one big window & street noise.

I'm to see the doctor at two forty-five & somehow
I arrive on time; the doctor sees me for ten minutes
& I sit down to wait for my zap at four-twenty.

What can you do? Just one of those things.
I slump into waiting mode, look around me.
A plump little old Inuk woman with a husband

who wears a blue surgical mask though whether
to keep germs out or in is making
those waiting around him uneasy.

She giggles & sings & shuffles a dance
to make him happy & here & there in the waiting room
faces light, mine included, not for the silly song

but just because the old woman is singing.

Wallet

Cancelled my transport, both ways,
a fit of independence.
Got downtown & realized I'd left my wallet behind.

All I had was backpack & Métro pass.
No money anywhere in the pockets, it seemed.
Only my whistle & bottled water between me & oblivion.

Took an Imodium an hour ago & forgot the rest.
What if that sudden gush returns?
And I'm supposed to drink three litres of water a day

so combine that just for fun
with a bladder & rectum excited by the rays
& you've got a dim idea of the ledges I dance along.

But I've made it this far, to the waiting room
where I sit waiting for the zap
but not really waiting,

there's this to do & when it's finished
it should all work itself out somehow
though I don't quite know how.

Holding Together

Neighbour's radio woke me 6 A.M.,
compromise reached by ten:
I not to bang doors at night

he not to turn his radio on till eight.
Breakfast I don't want to talk about,
got to get more water into me every day

if only to flush the toxins out,
but now with Sudden Urge Incontinence Syndrome
every step away from a public toilet

is a foolish step toward an illusion of freedom
(though I haven't got caught yet)
but took the Métro down & met Rick for lunch

at a sushi palace with chicken teriyaki on the side.

I've taken a gamble & so far no problem.
I'm holding together with ease & grace, but then

as in life, I could be involved anytime in my own end.

Grounded

Got to get out of this mire
talking about me more & more,
me & my gut, you know what I mean?

It's a mire of fire, I say
trying to remember every burning sensation
its approximate intensity, location, duration & meaning

to tell the doctor next time I see him
but it's hopeless unless I write it down
since I manage to forget most things I try to remember

& this isn't what I wanted to write about anyway,
any of this, all these antisocial details.
I want to fly, is what I want, & I'm not flying.

The Doors

I swim these days in languages & faces
blue aprons & white coats glimpsed as vision,
as the ongoing itself.

People loom & crystallize & fade
& already the burden of ceaseless loss & recognition
is turning me to silence again.

Wheelchair after wheelchair passes me by
pushed by orderlies & drivers & sons & daughters
pushed through automatic doors springing asunder

to reveal concrete & asphalt & stone of the mountainside
above the hospital & floor after floor
of the sick & injured the born & dying

in their moments of opening & passing through
into the flare of blue sky sun & wind just beyond
the heavy doors that release them.

Scattered Notes

A day of waiting, for rides, for treatment.
The past two days mostly throwing up & diarrhea.
Nausea may have inspired Sartre, but not me.

Why should I explain?
Perhaps because I've left some bloody chunks of me
back there in time & I'm explaining to them.

Misery as immediate now as happiness,
present when present, absent when gone.
Stuck on a toilet or over it,

vomiting or writing, whichever comes first.
Poetry of the moment may be a high art
but I haven't altogether got the hang of it yet.

Breath

As the malaise increases
I turn more & more to music
to the whistles & flutes

because they make me breathe
because they make me recognize my breath
because licked by forked flames of pain

they spin my breath into silver & gold.

Whistling In The Woods

In the little wood behind the residence
today the paths are full of men
gently exercising their damaged hearts

& I'm out here playing whistle to stay sane
flipping arpeggios around
when this guy comes up the path

I can't understand a word he says
but it looks like he likes the music,
in fact is in rapture over the sound in the trees,

his gestures large to include the sky
& ourselves standing there awkwardly glowing,
whistle & he & I —

we shake hands & move away —
as he turns to leave I play him
a bit of a Bach invention for the right hand.

This gets the nesting cardinals going
& we jam together for a little while
until I taper off & quit to listen to them

holding brilliant sway, invisible as ever.

Long Weekend

Back home again for the long weekend,
slept full in the absence of traffic noise

woke to a window with a grey doe out there
picking her way across a dew-wet field

so out on the porch steps in the sun
with my yogurt & banana

the cats weaving around us
Phoebe leaning on my leg

my only woman up against my other side
sharing warmth against the morning chill.

By all accounts the worst is yet to come
but right now I don't care, one way or the other.

The Residents

Saying goodbye around here
gets to be almost a habit.

We exchange addresses
never expecting to see again

or hear from some who become
statistics, shifting recollections

of a face, a veined hand on a Formica table
a shift in tone, a darkening of vocables,

of once brave words & wild laughter —
no matter whether it comes sooner or later

death comes & figuring that one out takes forever.

Coping

When I cough I have to press with left hand
to keep the coil of intestine in.

Yet the hemorrhoids haven't bled for four days now
& diarrhea has been replaced by constipation.

The burning in rectum has flamed out
because they stopped radiating there last week

oh yes & on the bus into town Sunday night
had to beg tolerance of my middle-aged male seat mate

for urinating into an empty fruit juice bottle
next to him, under my windbreaker

after quietly explaining my condition
which he took pretty well, if stiffly,

& all of this I put up with indefinitely & gladly
for each breath in turn.

Not Me

It's been days since I felt like walking up to the hospital
but every day after my time on the table
I ascend slowly into the wooded mountainside,

into green arches & enclosures
a ring of boulders around a certain rock to sit on
a place to rest & drink water.

If I wait awhile I'll even want to play
& through the trees & back again
the whistle's voice will come from everywhere

& nowhere too, breath & fingers playing, not me.

Waiting

Sitting in my clean beige residence room
I am not thinking in English
I am not thinking in French.

I am not thinking.
I am not playing whistle or flute
& I am not dreaming.

I am waiting for the lunchroom to open.
I glance once at my watch
& I am due to be zapped at one-thirty downtown

so this'll be the last line.

All Metaphor

Down to counting the days over & over
yet step into the woods behind the residence
& there's a robin song to listen to,

between two notes, starts somewhere, ends somewhere else.
A pink trillium on the path to wonder about,
last week in green light luminous, today withered.

It's all metaphor, a friend now dead once said
& so he loved metaphor.
What else was there to do?

Priestesses

The young women in white who burn me
are priestesses of their machine
moving chastely about my supine form

speaking numbers to one another
carefully laying a towel across my thighs
then delicately pulling my gown out from under

to expose a strip of me across the pubic bone
(& tactfully nothing lower)
around which the huge machine will turn & zap

belly & hips, the body I more & more become,
with invisible rays, beams
I must accept but never see,

all this in darkness
everybody but me behind a lead wall
while I am crisscrossed by flames I must believe in

after which the lights come on,
the beautiful young priestesses
help me sit up. We smile & say goodbye

until tomorrow, same time
& I retreat, clutching gown to bum
all the way to the changing room,

understanding that I've been touched.

Faith

Now is the beginning of watch & wait,
tests & analyses of tests
monitoring my waning side effects.

Now is the void, the not knowing,
knowing I will never know for sure
if one or a few rogue cells growing

might suddenly from hiding one day
burst out in limitless hungry adolescence.
I take things now each moment to its own

in faith that from not knowing, knowing comes.

Song, Sort Of

My butt inflamed with radiation burn
my glutei maxima having evolved to let me sit & think,
yet I don't sit down for a long time anywhere.

I'm not thinking about anything for long, either
but I'm home, I'm home again
& coming in the window from somewhere, robin song.

I'm just home, that's all. Home.

From Here

A narrow view through half-drawn blinds,
a bank of green leaves lit by a rainy day

from which translucent stems
spread to hold up tiny flowers.

Above them a shed wall weathers
& makes the bright edge of a dark open door.

Above them, a tangle of sharp elbows & knees,
a lowering apple bough.

Above them, branch & trunk of hawthorn,
& through the thorns a bit of sky.

Side Effects

Side effects slowly diminishing
V & me in bed together warm in morning
& wonderful! still no dysfunction

But I think the trick is not to think
too much about it,
but to stay warm & cuddle together

while this wild little rebellion in me
is put down (at some cost to the local scenery)
& dies away under cobalt energies

combined with love like this
to raise our temperatures
& other things as well.

A Kind Of Music

Back from radio & surgery consultations
another shot in the belly & the rip in the groin hurts

but that's not new & nobody cares right now
including me & even that isn't new,

this hovering over my body
this float of wings over the indignity of it all

whose wings they were & are
told in whispers by persons unseen.

Moments of no pain gather & pool
& reflect the face before I was born.

Is it really mine? No telling:
a kind of music passes through the air

belongs to no one & it's foolish to ask.
Enough that when my eyes open, there's light there.

Walking Out Again

Walking out again into a world folks think they know
is partly to step into bright glare,
partly a step backward into shadow.

Nobody knows what you've been through
& you're tired of talking about it anyway
though can't say why

can't say the reality of it
the luminous tones in flowers
backlit by setting sun

don't want to say
when at once you can taste & see
& not have to say anything.

All is present to the mind all the time.
What it chooses to take & hold to
is arbitrary as the blush of a petal.

The flower has a plan.
The petal has none & now
you are just another petal in the spring wind.

Birds

Hot days, the birds are under cover,
relinquish their extra dimension of space
to a sun pouring light through cloud.

Midday, no bird chatter,
just flitting shapes of shade in shade
flipping dead leaves over, scarfing up grubs,

good protein for flying days.
Warm air expands, air pressure drops,
we flap a lot & get nowhere.

Stay in the shade & wait for high pressure
when there's substance to fly in
& you fly high, fly, just fly.

Downpour

Heavy rain from 2 A.M. to now, mid-morning.
Phoebe follows me into my studio
& I have to force her out from under my desk

& onto the doormat, bristling with prickly fibres
which she dislikes but lies down on
while in large silvery blobs it rains outside.

Light is low & green out there. Leaves glisten.
Rain sound everywhere & nowhere
over this mountain slope descending

into a valley already rich in water.
Phoebe is now off the mat & on the floor
cutting in half my chair's rolling room

but she's closer now, too.
My hand drops to her wet curls
& her muzzle rises into my hand.

We are rich & not just in water.

Vow

Wanting the wide gaze my eyes as child had
I've done my share of yearning
before the hereafter & after the before

but haven't always let in what is here:
this blade of grass, this sudden wing or smile
this river of awarenesses we agree to call time

which I yearn to be released from
but will not, because the way out is into it
in full light of the jewel in every heart,

a way to bring forth the child of long ago.

3 A.M.

Up each night three or four times, down from twelve
which is progress, but not right either.
Is it getting better? Yes, but slowly.

You know all healing is slow at this age,
but then when things start not healing at all
you will be face-to-face

not with death, but with the part about dying:
the frightened old woman in you who refuses & refuses,
the old man who abuses because abused.

Such images take root in your mind.
No reason to respect these shells of life except
still human, young once, possibly beautiful

now they are fragile shacks of fear,
husks of emptiness, empty often
even of the knowledge of their emptiness

swept away in a river of blankness
where time is a jumble of times
all out of sequence & changing so fast

it hurts the eye within to look at it,
but there it is & you need to be ready.
There it all is, at three in the morning.

The Other Way

Yesterday the test results came back:
prostate specific antigen at zero point one,
testosterone zero. Hot flashes continue.

A DRI found the prostate 'small & smooth'
& I still get erections & enjoy what follows
so it's all good news & yay & hallelujah

& tears brim up from the paradox behind my eyes
because I know that some of those
I lived with during the worst days

kind to me & kind to each other
are going the other way.
I too will fail if I don't remember them,

old men hobbling & patient under indignities,
brave & funny baldheaded women.
I wonder if I don't owe them my life.

I know I owe them something big.

Stitches

Major focus on pain these days
what with these subcutaneous stitches
pulling unpredictably suddenly

a stinging & burning combined
a flash of pain that stops everything
mid-gesture, mid-sentence

mid-everything
so there are no trains of thought these days
only six-nanosecond bytes.

Don't expect a story out of this:
the sting of the stitches persists
at random intervals,

no consistent patterns of movement
trigger the twinges.
I'm on the long retreat from Moscow here.

The raiders gallop across our line,
take a few lives, a few horses
then disappear in fury & thunder.

That's me all right, hunkered down,
face in the slush of the march,
getting up carefully, afterwards.

Among Trees

But that's not the end, not yet.
What happens, happens before these eyes
& you change it, like water into wine, to words.

For instance, right now.
Lying on a bed in a room with yellow walls
close your eyes & you are among saplings & weeds

below house & field
along overgrown tractor roads
thence to the cool of the tall woods.

Seeing the straight thick trunks soar
to a green canopy of leaves far overhead
you want to be there,

even hobbling, clutching yourself.
What's a little selfish pain after all
when you could be out there, among trees?

Autumn

We call it a touch of autumn in the air.
What to call it better, I don't know, maybe
summer's fullness being pulled from everywhere

as the planet turns over & I don't,
as day by day something is drawn from me
that I must doubt will return.

Spring & its greening speak to what's new
yet what is leaving me is old & sustaining
& in between winter gapes, another gap in time.

Too many of these indefinite antecedents.
Even while I was on my back two weeks indoors
the mountain has blazed up red from deep green

& I'm left out of synch again
with the general turnover of the planet
but truth is I'm singing & however odd the song

I'll sing it as long as I can stand to sing.

Hologram

On the screen, the uncut arc of curving grass blade tip
holds a clear water drop
& in its lens & mirror, the world inverts.

The world is always flashing at us upside down
second by second, leaf by leaf,
drop by trembling crystal drop.

This one, caught in lens & digital information,
will never fall, never leave the green tip,
will be held in code as long as code lasts.

We need to see what we see,
not look past but through each meeting
to the universal jewel it might contain.

The pictures on the screen
change faster & faster. Too bad
to have to find happiness by lens & screen,

in a red-tailed dragonfly digitized on a bud tip,
in a necklace of dewy spider web information,
in a misty receding cathedral of tall tree representations.

Many paths, many visions, all illusory.
The miracle is open to any, not on a screen
but in our own eyes & ears & voices

discovering just in time what we have to lose.

Sweet Spot Song

There's no going back, once you reach

the whorehouse of whenever, wherever, whatever.

So be it, that's the bitter end of the world

you know it & I know it

what's harder to come by is the sweet end

which is why everybody eats so much sugar

to fill the void of despair

& don't tell me you don't do it & know it

but how about going back to sweet as metaphor

for neat skills of hand, children's faces,

lovers in their generosity,

things going right when we let them,

finding the sweet spot when we can?

A Year Of Cancer

Have I ever said right out how much joy there was
in those days of sheer uncertainty?
Everything I saw, I saw sharp & clear

everything I heard, touched, felt was sacred,
illuminated from within & we were all saints
in various stages of development.

That was then, now is now.
The sharpness dulls a little despite me;
my eyes soften their focus.

But still with me, here within
beating with my heart
sensing with my skin

truth lies under what happened to me,
what happens every day to someone, to many:
they learn they can die, can & will

so they turn & see & hear
& with no time to waste,
forgive all of it & just love.

I've known people to do this.

Passage

We heard her first thin cries this morning
lungs filling with world & air,

Anna, her new mother, exhausted
with the 25 hours since her waters broke,

Simon, the father, supportive, embracing,
murmuring love in her ear,

dhula, nurse, doctor, all women
& Vicki, a grandmother for the first time,

Moksha watching, holding, massaging her sister
& me, now a grandpa, all of us

just laughing, laughing to ourselves,
laughing just to laugh, silly as it sounds

while in the middle of all this,
against my daughter's breast

infant rose lips already seeking,
a perfectly formed unblemished miracle

girl child unto us had been born.

A Window In Winter

Birches white & leaning
into the general brown & grey

the one circle of clarity
surrounded by an edge of window frost

a wandering oval of distance & trees
embraced in crystal busywork

all the preoccupations of locked molecules
all their laws & rules

join & fuse & separate,
an urban tumult of egos & uses

& through it all, unrecognized, unrecognizable,
a translucence from the outer day,

that should tell us but only hints
at glories beyond any.

But so much for the frame:
out to the birches again, themselves

leaning, in the dusk seeming slowly to fall,
in the cold air, yet clear, so clear out there.

February

2

Every Moment Of Every Day

How many days has it been,
how many hours, minutes, seconds,
moments of conscious pain?

This has been a hurting time
crowding thought out of the brain
crowding senses & the space they witness

& even sometimes the light itself:
all goes to glare, to grey, to trembling hands
gripping the wound to close it & take it away.

I can say this, now I'm coming out of there
& looking back at those of you still going through,
some with no end in sight but death

earned with more of the same misery,
it's especially you I want to say this to,
what you may already know,

what anybody can find when they go through,
the heart within your anatomical heart,
the heart that's all that's left to you.

Anytime again, it could be me in there.
A part of me is still in there with you
& won't be free of pain until you are.

Floating World Again

If it weren't for conceptual mind
you would never know that the barn wall in sunlight
framed in a dazzle of snow

is a representation, a mock-up in your brain
& if you thought it was the real thing,
an illusion.

But there it is, in tones of weathered wood,
a delight to what you call your eye,
browns, greys, deep reds.

What to do with them, these ignorant
treasured dreams in which you live?
You are taken in by all this fool's gold,

yet richly here, offered to you.

Nirvana

I like this & you like that.
So, is one better? For you, for me?

I is a window.
Me is squatting & jumping around

in front of the window
crouching squalid squawking monkey cousin

or a tiny dot of self in a cold sea
always about to drown in it

all of which the window regards
neither with contempt nor without:

simply an outpouring of suchness
a window open to the light & air

as allows the air we breathe
& a necessary happiness.

The Secret Garden

Here is the secret garden of fools
of wastrels & poets busy destroying themselves

Here is the hell of not being able
to say what you mean in your own language

Here is dissent & consent, the yin & yang
contained in a waterdrop's moment

Here is the way of the way things are,
translucent, transcendent, transitory

Here is the first step of a ten thousand mile journey
& the last & the step after that

Here is where the fun begins & ends
& never ends, that's the trick of it, never ends.

The Moment Of Diagnosis

Out of nowhere, it hits.
You are an ant on a hot sidewalk
full of scurrying people

& a big foot slaps down on you
& the world you knew is gone
& there is no you to notice that

but you aren't an ant.
No little machine, you,
no you aren't. You are (fill in the blanks)

& you notice the colours are brighter & better yet
deeper & stranger,
& you not only understand the tragedy of the universe,

you accept it, eat it, drink it, the vision
of a meaningless death from the inside out
sometime in the time to come.

Would you give up this vision
for your former innocence, you ask of some
& nobody you ask would.

Always a little smile, a slow shake of the head.

Stormy Day

Today, deeper & richer shadows.
All glistens in wild storm rain,
the wet leaves plastered red & yolk yellow.

Went out a few times for a few minutes,
but nothing you could call a walk,
mostly from house to work hut & back

listening to the wind, then music within,
mind focused below thought, or above
& an open window to witness wind & mind,

the window of empty gaze it was there for.

November Letter

Water drops hang from thorn tips
& circle the grey light within
while each reflects the sky.

What is life like here?
What is life like anywhere?
What is life like?

Nothing. Like nothing other.
Like nothing else anywhere.
Summer weeds along the shed wall lie low,

yet their prostrate stalks glow in the rain.
Radiation still takes a lot of my get up & go
but so far leaves my eyes alone.

What I see of this cold dark landscape
warms me. My eyes feast on rich reds & browns
& I am fed. Life here is —

life, here, & good.

Not If But When

Some call it a scare,
a life interrupted, according to others

a scurry of ants you dig from their underground nest
antennas sensing, touching in the dark

then suddenly thrown into light,
blinds you at first, then exposes you to yourself

then illuminates all around you
& you are them & they are you

if you're lucky enough to be there,
really there, when it happens to you.

Small Rain

The plants that dominate the bank above this window,
impossible to remember the name,
are coming up tiny & green again.

In this rainy light they glow,
as does everything, weathered boards,
thorn tree bark, glistening rocks

& against the dark cavern of the tractor shed
a mist of drops glinting, their falling
bending & twisting in the currents of the air

both information & blessing.
I doubt that I'm the one doing the blessing,
but then I doubt everything, don't I?

Generally a rainy day is seen as grey,
but where's the grey here?
Do I see, or are there, riches everywhere?

Does it make a difference which is true?
The seedlings drink the water & the light
& I drink the light & the young shoots' green.

We are all rich in a moment beyond belief.

The Use Of

A few days perhaps before
lilac leaves grow large enough
to hide the branch that holds them

the black of the bark mixes
with a green translucence in the buds
in the early morning eye of the beholder

making waking up in light again astonishing.

Last Year's Garden

A hot spring morning in last year's garden
pulling up stakes & throwing out rocks,
collecting bottomless tin cans

that kept tomato seedlings safe
from cutworms & such.
Bits of red yarn that tied up the plants

could get wound around
the turning shafts of the tiller
& stop everything,

so all must be picked up,
so Claude can ride in on his ride-on tractor
& till everything

while I retreat to the house
& lie still so the sweat can evaporate
& body & shirt dry out.

Strange to be tired this early.
Not used to stooping & bending
& thinking over last year's garden.

Could just be the hot work or maybe
the thinking, maybe the cancer again,
who knows? Who cares just now?

Here

Something different about the foliage here,
the greens deeper, sink more into the heart

& tasseled maple flowers in the wind, seen,
take your breath & all goes almost still,

still in your nature from one time to the next,
in a flood of riches wherever you look.

Anyway something is different,
a shift in the spectra or the seeing,

no real difference compared to the difference
between living & not

& that's the real difference,
here & living along with green leaves, or not.

Mountain Dog

That Phoebe. She's got me to let her in again
away from the heat she still suffers in summer
though we clipped her shaggy coat to three centimeters

& here she is again when I come in from out of doors,
flat on her cushion, flounder eyes rolling up at me,
clearly apprehensive but not one to push or beg.

Of course I let her stay in where
it's darker & cooler than summer out there.
She should be panting a thin high cold air

not this humid lowland syrup of thick breath & mist.
She lifts a languid foreleg from her snowy chest
to let me know I can give her a tummy rub.

What can I do?
Among others, I belong to her.

What Can Happen When You Find Out

Each event you see, really see
comes with correspondingly inward seeing.
Every encounter illuminates.

A certain curl in the bark of a tree
manifests how it grew that way,
a stone's scars, evidence of aeons.

You look up at the sky
& you are seeing into space,
seeing the stars in their inconceivable distances.

Not a surround sound screen for your amusement,
there is more to everything around
& you are utterly wherever it is you are.

Whoever it is, you are too:
a depth to everyone around you,
a sweetness folded into silence.

Raspberry

Here, there, through green multitudes of leaves
a red stab of a raspberry to the eye
out of reach among prickles & thorns

no matter the thought of sweetness
no matter the knowledge that comes
with tongue's slow crush of berry on palate,

the slide of tastes down the throat
so beside itself with pleasure
it forgets to whom it belongs

takes command & orders me
to wade into the bush in shorts
& take the stings & itches for the point

in time & space & reach, when between
finger & thumb & gentle pull, the raspberry
yields to mouth & mind.

Awe

Thunderstorm last night,
even now the sky's bruised blue

& all beneath it
waiting for the next one-two,

white flash fading to violet,
bright roar of all that's true.

ECO-AUDIT
*Printing this book using Rolland Enviro 100 Book
instead of virgin fibres paper saved the following resources:*

Trees	Solid Waste	Water	Air Emissions
1	71 kg	4,698 L	185 kg